HOW TO WRITE
REPORTS

ANNE FAUNDEZ

QEB Publishing, Inc.

QEB

Copyright © QEB Publishing, Inc. 2007

First published in the United States by
QEB Publishing, Inc.
23062 La Cadena Drive
Laguna Hills, CA 92653

www.qeb-publishing.com

Library of Congress Control Number:
2007000927

ISBN 978-1-59566-345-0

Written by Anne Faundez
Designed by Jackie Palmer
Editor Louisa Somerville
Illustrations by Tim Loughead

Publisher Steve Evans
Creative Director Zeta Davies
Senior Editior Hannah Ray

Printed and bound in China

Words in **bold** are explained
in the glossary on page 30.

CONTENTS

NONFICTION TEXTS

When you write about yourself and the world around you, giving information, facts, and sometimes personal opinions, you are writing nonfiction. There are all sorts of nonfiction texts. A newspaper report, a **resume**, a **review**, a balanced argument, a **recount** of a vacation, and a project on the rain forest are all examples of nonfiction writing.

Purpose

The words you use and how you present your writing depends on what sort of nonfiction you want to write. Are you writing for a school newspaper? If so, you need a catchy **headline**. Are you doing a project about the Ancient Greeks? If so, you need to organize the information under **subheadings**, with each subheading introducing a new aspect of the topic.

Audience

Who will be reading what you've written? If your writing is intended for your friends, then you can use language with which they are familiar and **contractions**, such as "doesn't" and "won't." If your writing is for your teacher or someone you don't know, then you should use formal language—"will not," for example—and avoid words like "great" and "cool."

A class diary is an example of a nonfiction text.

glue stick

Class Diary
My birthday treat
by Leonie Smith

June 10th
For my birthday, my dad took me to visit Zone Studios on Saturday. Galaxy Gorgons, my favourite film, was made here.
In the first building were the sets from some of the scenes. In one corner, we even saw the gorgons' spaceship! We entered a workshop where people were working on a model of a monstrous one-eyed fish. Maybe this character will star in the next Galaxy film!

Then we went into the props and costumes department—and saw the necklace with extra-sensory powers! Finally, we passed through a room full of computers where people were playing with on-screen graphics. This was the best birthday treat ever.

THEY CAME FROM OUTER SPACE...

the Galaxy Gorgons

STARRING

Researching

Nonfiction writing is about facts, so you need to research your topic. Talk to people with knowledge or experience, and use books or the Internet. Keep a writer's notebook full of facts to use when you write. Make sketches, too, if you like.

Tip

Nobody gets a piece of writing right the first time around. You need to plan and prepare an outline, either as a diagram or chart, or as a list, before writing.

Once you've written a **draft**, you may want to use a word-processing program to move **paragraphs** around or to do a **spell-check**.

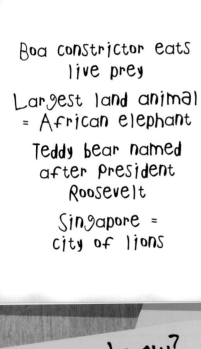

Boa constrictor eats live prey

Largest land animal = African elephant

Teddy bear named after President Roosevelt

Singapore = city of lions

Here are some good Websites to use when you are doing your research:

www.aolatschool.com/students

www.kidsclick.org

www.enchantedlearning.com

Did you know?

Leonardo da Vinci filled his notebooks with sketches of all sorts of things: a bird's wing, devices to make water flow, hats. He also did mirror writing, which is going backward across the page, to form a mirror image of his normal writing.

WRITING ABOUT A TRIP

When you create a piece of writing that relates the details of an event, you are recounting that event. Suppose you went on a school trip and your teacher has asked you to write about it. The best way to do this is to describe the events as you experienced them.

Starting to write

Present the events in **chronological order.** Describe briefly the place you were visiting so that the reader can get a flavor for it. Because you are the person who experienced everything, write from your point of view, either using the pronoun "I" or, if you were with your class or friends, "we." Make your writing interesting by adding your own observations and feelings.

Which tense?

You should write in the past tense because you are describing events that have already taken place.

All in order

Before you start, it's helpful to draw a time line. Write down the events of the trip in the order in which they happened—from start to finish. You only need to write key words or abbreviations that will help you recount the information.

Transitional words show the sequence of events:

- First
- Next
- Then
- Shortly after
- Later
- Finally

Start with a sentence that sets the scene.

Each paragraph explains a different event in chronological order.

Try to include some unusual facts to keep your reader interested.

Notes for trip to Miramar
Guide—Tunnel—Reefs (coral)—
Coast (Sharks!)—Shipwreck—Danger zone
(snakes)—Talk

Give your piece of writing a title that tells the reader what it is about.

Break the text into paragraphs to make it easier to read.

Our trip to the aquatic life center

Today we visited the Miramar Aquatic Life Center. Our bus pulled up right as it was opening. Our guide was waiting for us inside. We followed him through a transparent tunnel surrounded by the ocean. There were real-life fish swimming right up to us.

First, we visited the Reefs Sanctuary, with hundreds of rainbow-colored fish darting in and out of red and pink coral. After that, we moved on to the Coast Sanctuary, which had huge stingrays, turtles, sharks, and even a shipwreck. One shark came swimming right up to me. I had never been face to face with a shark before, and I was glad that I was safe in the tunnel, away from its huge teeth.

Next, we visited the Danger Zone. It had sea snakes and gigantic jellyfish.

After lunch, we listened to a seminar about the fish we'd seen. It was really interesting. Did you know that the jellyfish has no brain?

By the time we'd finished, we were tired and ready for the ride home, but it had been a great day!

After recounting the events, end with a closing **statement.**

Springboard

Recount the events of a family outing or a trip to a museum. Begin by making a time line of the main events. Don't forget to use transitional words (first, next, and so on).

NEWSPAPER REPORT

Newspaper reports have to grab the reader's attention. They need punchy headlines and a gripping first few lines to make sure that you read on. News stories cover everything from world events to lost puppies. You can turn just about anything that happens to you into a news report.

News style

Flip through some newspaper **articles** and you'll see that they have things in common:

> The headline (title) is set in large type. It consists of only a few words—just enough to catch the reader's eye.

the daily news

WALKING SHARK

Scientists discover a shark in the coral reefs off Indonesia that can walk on its fins

By Shar Kattak

A team of scientists has discovered many new species of fish and coral around the islands of Indonesia—including a fish that can walk.

Legging it
The shark is just over a meter long, with a slender body. It uses its pectoral fins as "legs" to walk along the ocean floor in search of food. Sam Sebastian, a leading member of the team, said, "They're extraordinary animals that sort of walk on their fins. They spend a lot of time on the bottom looking for mussels and crabs."

Watch the birdie
The coastal area, known as Bird's Head, is home to more than 1,200 species of fish and almost 600 types of coral.

> The introduction is one or two sentences long and says what the article is about.

> The place where the name of the person who wrote the article appears is known as the byline.

> The paragraphs are arranged under subheadings.

> The text is broken into short paragraphs.

What to write?

Try writing a news report about something that has happened to you recently—the day your mom went to work in her slippers or when your school won a prize, for example. To catch the reader's eye you need an attention-grabbing headline. Make sure that it describes what your article is about. Use rhyme, **alliteration**, or even puns—and keep it short!

Tackling the facts

A newspaper report describes what happened, who was involved, and when, how, and where the event took place. Introduce the subject in the first paragraph. In the next paragraph build on what you have said, adding supporting facts, background information, and **quotes**. Put less important details at the end of your article. For example, you might start with:

JONES' JOURNEY JEOPARDY
Ten-year-old Aaron Jones had a brush with danger on his way to school.

Headline uses alliteration.

First line makes you want to read on.

Tip

Use a computer to lay out your article in the style of a newspaper **column**. Vary the **fonts**, setting the headline in the largest font size and in **bold**. You'll need to **edit** your article to make it fit in the column.

Writing style

Make your article exciting by varying your writing style.

- Follow a short sentence with a longer one.
- Use active verbs ("a storm lashed the town"), not passive ones ("the town was lashed by a storm").
- Introduce different points of view by using quotes from the people involved.
- Divide your writing into paragraphs of three or four sentences.
- **Use subheadings.**
- Break up your story with illustrations—either photos or drawings—and informative **captions**.

Did you know?

Newspapers have been around for a very long time. In Ancient Rome, the government kept its citizens informed about things like war or the emperor's health by way of handwritten news sheets. These were placed in market squares where everyone could go and read them.

Springboard

Rewrite a nursery rhyme or fairy tale as a newspaper report. Here's a headline to get you started: "Eggs-hausting," says Humpty Dumpty.

AN INTERVIEW

An interview is a meeting with someone to ask them questions, either about themselves or about a special topic. The interviewer is the person who asks the questions and the interviewee is the person who answers them. The interviewer takes notes and then writes them up as a nonfiction text.

Tip

Always ask permission before you start your interview.

Who to interview?

You might want to ask a local author about their writing, question your grandparents about life 50 years ago, or even find out what your neighbors think about the shopping mall that's just opened nearby.

Preparing an interview

Make a list of all the things you'd like to find out. If you are interviewing people about their past, your questions might be about the clothes they wore, the music they enjoyed, their former hobbies, or even how they got to school in the morning. Make sure you phrase your questions so that the person is encouraged to speak, and not give "yes" or "no" answers.

Interview with Daz Dayman

Q. How did you feel when you got home?
A. v. happy & good 2 c my cats. Not v. much time 2 relax bc next album 2 rcd.

Q. What do you think about a reunion?
A. wd like 2 c band m'bers agn

Q. What sort of music did you listen to?
A.

Q. What was it like...?
A.

Q. Tell me about...
A.

Abbreviate words as you write down answers.

Allow enough of a gap to write down your interviewee's answers.

ACTIVITY

Write down the questions on a notepad, leaving plenty of space between each one. Use this blank space to write down your interviewee's answers.

Tip

Take notes when you're writing down what your interviewee says, because you can't write as fast as they speak. Abbreviate words—just like you do when you're texting. Write "lk" for "like" and "tdy" for "today." Leave out all small words, such as "a" and "the." Use an ampersand (&) for "and."

Interviewing

Now that you have a list of questions, you need to find the right person to answer them. If your project is about life in the 1950s, the best people to interview are older people. If you want to find out what people think about the new shopping mall, ask people who live in the area. Try to write down as much as you can so that you will be able to convey the character of your interviewee.

Writing the interview

Begin your interview with an introduction, saying who the interviewee is and what the interview is about. Set up your interview like a playscript, with a new line for each speaker. Make the interview sound as if the interviewee is talking by using the actual words he or she used. Don't forget to replace your abbreviations with full words!

Begin a new line for each speaker.

Use initials to show who is speaking.

Include expressions that the interviewee uses, such as "um," "er," and "oh," to make it sound as though they're speaking.

BEATLES' FAN ELLA EVANS TALKS TO HER NIECE, KIM, ABOUT GROWING UP IN THE 1960s.

KE: What did you like and dislike about school?

EE: My favorite class was geography. I loved learning about other countries. In those days, we didn't go on vacation far away, so even learning about Ohio seemed exotic! My least favorite subject was sewing. It would take me the whole lesson just to thread a needle!

KE: What did you want to be when you were my age?

EE: When I saw a man walk on the moon for the first time, I was so impressed that I wanted to be an astronaut.

KE: What sort of music did you like?

EE: My favorite music was rock-'n'-roll—oh, and anything by The Beatles.

Springboard

Make a list of questions you'd like to ask one of the following people:

- your favorite pop star
- a sports hero
- Christopher Columbus
- a character from a book

BOOK REVIEW

A review is a report in which you give your opinion about things like a book, film, CD, concert, play, or an exhibition.

Write a book review

How you write will depend on whether you are reviewing a **fiction** or nonfiction book. However, your review should always start with the title of the book, the name of the author, and, if the book has pictures, the name of the illustrator or photographer.

Review a story or picture book

Tell the reader where the story takes place and describe the main characters. Write about the characters' relationships to each other. Are they friends from school or did they meet through some strange coincidence? Describe the **plot**—but not in too much detail. Now give your opinion of the book. What do you like about the story? Is the plot convincing? Are the characters believable? Is it a book that you couldn't put down? If the book has illustrations, what did you like about them? Did they reflect the mood of the book?

Say what the book is about.

Put the title of the book, the author, and the illustrator at the top.

Mr. Whizz's School of Magic

by Ebony Lee
Illustrated by Jo Melon

This story is about a group of pupils at Mr. Whizz's school for wizards. Most classes involve boring experiments such as how to turn a pea into a pumpkin. But one day, Mr. Whizz walks into the classroom with a brand-new book of spells. From that moment on, life changes dramatically, especially for star pupils Jazz and Glitter—and, of course, for Mr. Whizz.

My favorite characters are Mr. Whizz, who is always forgetting things, and Glitter, who is warmhearted, witty, and funny.

The black-and-white drawings have a lot of detail and depict the characters just as I imagined them.

I would recommend this book to anyone who enjoys a good laugh.

Mention your favorite character.

Who are the main characters?

Say what you liked about the story.

What do you think of the illustrations?

Don't give away the ending. If your review has been successful, the readers will want to find out for themselves.

Review a nonfiction book

Reviewing a nonfiction book is a little different. Write a **summary** of the contents. Describe the way the book is organized. Does it have a **glossary** and an **index**? Does it have photos or diagrams to support the text? Now give your opinion of the book. Is it clearly written? Does it hold your interest and tell you what you wanted to know? Are the photographs eye-catching and informative? Do you know more about the topic after having read the book? Does the book make you want to read more about the topic?

Springboard

The best reviews are those that are written with enthusiasm. Review a film or a CD about which you feel strongly. This is important because if you write about something that you don't particularly like or dislike, what you write will be halfhearted. If you find it boring, it'll be hard not to make your review sound dull, too.

Put the title of the book, the author, and the photographer at the top.

Endangered Animals
By Joshua Squire
Photographs by Tammy Wayne

How are the contents organized?

Say what the book is about.

The book looks at animals from every continent that are in danger of extinction.

The book is divided into sections, one for each continent. Five types of animals—mammals, fish, birds, reptiles, and insects—are examined in each section. Under "Australia," for example, you will find pages on the koala, saltwater crocodile, giant dragonfly, turquoise parrot, and lungfish. The text is divided up using subheadings. Underneath each one are facts about the animal and threats to its habitat.

Describe photos and charts.

The book has many large, beautiful photos. There's a map at the beginning of each section that shows where each animal comes from.

Mention any special features.

The book is well organized and clearly written, with an index so that you can find facts easily. It is so informative that it makes me want to find out more about the topic.

What did you like about the book?

13

BALANCED REPORT

A balanced report presents both sides of an argument and is usually made up of facts, or a mix of fact and opinion. Often the topic is **controversial**, with people either for or against it.

What's the purpose?

There are several reasons for writing a balanced report:

- To show that there are two sides to an argument.
- To give readers all the information they need to make up their minds about where they stand on an issue.
- To have all the facts in front of you before you take sides in a debate.

Facts, facts, facts

You'll need to research your topic thoroughly to find out the facts for and against each argument before writing your report. Your research might include:
- Finding facts on the Internet or in your local library.
- Conducting a **survey** or **questionnaire**.
- Interviewing people.

Writing style

When you write your report, use the present tense ("need" instead of "needed") and use **impersonal language** ("it was found" instead of "we found").

ACTIVITY

Try preparing a balanced report. There's a rumor flying around that a theme park is going to be built just outside your town. Some of your friends favor this proposal, while others are against it. You're not sure where you stand, so you need to gather all the facts. What arguments can you come up with, for and against?

Useful words

However • On the one hand/ On the other hand • Therefore • Then • To sum up • To conclude

Springboard

Choose one of these topics and produce a list of arguments for and against it. Try to have the same number of points in each column.

- Should school uniforms be mandatory?
- Is tourism good for a country?
- Should zoos exist?
- Is reality TV entertainment?

Tip

Use bullet points for each new argument. This will make the information easier to read.

Begin with an opening statement to tell the reader what the report is about.

CLASS REPORT

SHOULD THERE BE MORE SPORTS DURING THE SCHOOL DAY?

Our class reports on the arguments for and against introducing more sports during the school day.

Use impersonal language and the present tense.

REMEMBER TO:

List "for" and "against" arguments in separate columns.

Write a point in favor of the argument and a point against it.

FOR

- Children need more exercise, especially because they spend their free time watching TV and playing video games.

- Being overweight is a growing problem.

- There's too much time spent on subjects such as math, so children who are good at other things, like sports, lose out.

AGAINST

- It's not up to the school to provide more sports. Parents need to get their children to be more active.

- It would be better to spend more time teaching children about healthy eating.

- To cover the all the subjects, the school day would have to be lengthened.

End your report with a statement summing up both arguments or stating which argument you agree with.

Place the "for" and "against" arguments alongside each other so that they roughly match up.

To sum up, after reading the arguments, our class believes that it would be a good idea for children to play more sports during the school day.

SPORTS REPORT

Suppose that you've been asked to write about a school sports event—a swim meet, the football finals, or a field day race, such as the 100-meter dash or even the egg-and-spoon race. How can you make your writing grab the reader's attention?

Starting to write

Here are some tips for good sports reporting:

- Keep sentences short and avoid **explanatory clauses**. For example, instead of writing "All eyes were on Hari, who, as well as being really popular, was the school's best sprinter," you could say "All eyes were on Hari. He was the school's best sprinter. He was also really popular."

- Use an **active voice**. ("Ben pounded the ground.") A **passive voice** ("The ground was pounded by Ben.") will slow down your writing.

- Use **metaphors** and **similes**—"Anya was a white streak in the distance," "Misha raced like the wind."

- Build mood. For example, describe the suspense before the race. Which of the entrants looked nervous/confident? Were the spectators noisy with excitement or hushed with suspense? You could also describe key moments of tension—the moment when Jay's dog slipped out of its collar one minute into the race and ran onto the track, almost making her fall.

Springboard

Write a report about your school team's most recent competition. (Choose any team sport, such as soccer or basketball.) Write the report as if you are writing for a local newspaper and the team members are local sports stars. Include quotes from the team and from their manager, of course.

ACTIVITY

Choose a sport to write about. How are you going to present it? Are you going to start with the result, "Anna wins by a whisker"? Or do you wish to keep your audience in suspense until the very end? If so, describe the sequence of events as they happen.

United win
by Joshua Squire

A brilliant strike by newcomer Fernando saves the day for reigning champions, United. With no goals scored, United seemed content with a tie. But with just five minutes to go, Fernando saw his chance and grabbed the ball.

In for the kill

He cruised his way down the field and skillfully fought off one opponent after another. With a superb throw, he winged the ball home. "I never thought I'd do it," he said triumphantly.

> Use adjectives, but use them sparingly because too many will slow down the pace of your writing.

> Organize your writing into short paragraphs to make it easier to read and hold the reader's interest.

> Use a subheading to introduce a new idea.

> Use powerful verbs—for "ran," say "galloped" or "sprinted."

> Use quotes from competitors and spectators to back up your statements.

Dull or exciting?

Here are two reports on the same event, but one is boring while the other grabs your attention. What makes the difference?

Record finish in freestyle finals
by V. Dull

The freestyle race began. The lead was taken by Emma, who was in lane 1 and whose dive placed her in front. She swam through the water quickly.
Then, from lane 3, Verna came forward. She swam through the water, moving with strong strokes.

Record finish in freestyle finals
by V. Exciting

Splash! They were off! Emma, in lane 1, was off to a great start. Her long dive put her into the lead. She glided effortlessly through the water, leaving behind a froth of bubbles like a speed boat.
Then Verna streaked forward from lane 3. Soon she was inching her way to the finish with swift strokes that barely rippled the water's surface.

- explanatory clauses
- active voice
- powerful verb
- simile
- boring adjectives
- repetition
- exciting adjective

RECOUNTING EVENTS IN DIFFERENT STYLES

Very often, what we write and how we write it depends on who we are writing for. For example, you would use one style of writing to describe a theme park visit to your best friend and a different style of writing to describe it to your teacher.

Informal style

Your best friend Nadine loves going to the theme park. You'd write to her in a relaxed style—almost as if you were talking to her. You'd take for granted that she already knows a lot of things about the theme park, so you wouldn't have to explain as much to her.

FUN PARK
ADMIT ONE

FUN PARK
ADMIT ONE

REMEMBER TO USE:

25 Diamond Lane
Pleasant, VA 22944

November 20, 2007

Dear Nadine,
    I went to Adventure Towers yesterday with Mom, Dad, and Susie. The bus ride took forever (as usual). The rides were fantastic and there was a gigantic new rollercoaster that you're going to love. I thought it'd be scary, but it was awesome.
    For lunch we had hamburgers and that ice cream you love. Yum! In the afternoon, we went on a water ride. You should have seen Dad—he got soaked. Mom couldn't stop laughing.
    We had a really cool day. I'll ask Mom if we can go again when you're back from vacation.
    Love,
    Jane x x x

relaxed, informal style

colloquial language ("scary" and "awesome")

small pieces of information about the writer

exclamation marks for emphasis

contractions ("you're" instead of "you are")

Formal style

Your teacher asks you to write about your day at the theme park for a display of work aimed at parents. As you don't know the people you're writing for, the language you use should be more formal. You need to give more details since they may not know the theme park. To help the reader, you could include some subheadings.

Give facts rather than personal opinions.

My trip to Adventure Towers

Yesterday, my parents took my sister and me to Adventure Towers, <u>the largest theme park in this part of the country</u>. It is not always easy to find parking there, so we took a bus.

All sorts of rides

We tried out many different rides. Then we went on the new rollercoaster. It was huge, and it had a lot of cars with four seats across each row. It was frightening but also great fun.

Water everywhere

We had lunch in a restaurant overlooking the lake. After lunch, we went on a water ride that took us up and down slides and through tunnels. We were completely wet by the end of the ride.

Time to go home

We were too tired to do much more after the water ride. Luckily we <u>did not</u> have to wait too long for the bus back into town. We all enjoyed ourselves and had a very exciting day.

Use formal language.

ACTIVITY

Write recounts of a birthday party you've enjoyed for two people from this list:

- grandparent
- younger brother or sister
- pen pal
- school newspaper editor

Springboard

Keep a diary. Each day, recount the day's events. Decide if you'll write in an informal or formal style. If your diary is "for your eyes only." you may choose an informal style. However, if you want others to read it, you should be more formal.

WRITING A RESUME

A resume gives factual information about your education, achievements, and hobbies. It can help employers decide if you are the best person for a job. A resume can also help determine if you should be given an award.

Did you know?

A resume is also called a CV. CV stands for "curriculum vitae," which means "the story of your life" in Latin.

Is a resume the same as an autobiography?

A resume gives facts about what a person has done in their life. The facts are usually placed in reverse order with the most recent first.

An autobiography is the story of someone's life, written by that person. It includes observations, feelings, facts, and opinions. It is written in the first person. The story is often relayed in chronological order.

Writing a resume

It's important to keep your resume short and to the point. Don't forget that the person reading it will also be reading lots of other resumes. Here are some tips:

- Begin by writing your name, date of birth, and contact details.
- List all the things you've done, both in and out of school. Start with your most recent achievement.
- Include as many things as you can that are relevant to what you are applying for. You need to persuade the person that you are the most appropriate candidate.
- List your favorite hobbies and pastimes.

Do include in your resume achievements such as:
- I was awarded a gold swimming medal.
- My painting was selected for a competition.
- I helped organize a flea market for charity.

DON'T include facts like these in your resume:
- My cat loves cheese.
- My pencil case is blue.
- I failed my math test.

Research a celebrity of your choice (living or dead) and write their resume for them, listing their achievements and hobbies.

Springboard

Put your name at the top. Centering the type on the page looks good.

Toby Mann

Date of birth: April 4,1998
Address: 19 Main Street, Goodtown, TX 10930
Telephone: (212) 434-5678

List your educational achievements starting with the most recent.

Education:
April 2007: Passed Piano Playing and Composition with honors

January 2007: Won third prize in Goodtown's Music Festival

December 2006: Played the Tin Man in school production of *The Wizard of Oz*

May 2005: Took part in interview about my school, published in the *Goodtown Gazette*

Hobbies:
Skateboarding, music, reading

Include the names of two people who can recommend you when you apply for a job.

References:
Mrs. P. Shooter (918) 954-1234
Mr. C. Saw (918) 954-3465

Tip

Type your resume on a computer. It looks neater and it can be easily updated and altered.

POWER OF PERSUASION

Some writing tries to persuade the reader to agree with what is being said and gives only one point of view. For example, a brochure advertising a vacation in a mountain home "with magnificent views of the lake" avoids saying that you can only see the lake if you stand on a chair. A tempting advertisement for an MP3 player claims that you can tune in to live performances, but doesn't state that first you must buy an expensive card to put into the player.

Twinkletoes
does the dancing for you!

Want to become a fantastic dancer in just TWO minutes? Then strap some Twinkletoes onto your shoes and get tapping.

You'll be a whirling, twirling dance star and the envy of your friends.

Twinkletoes are the latest innovation in dance technology.

Full money-back guarantee if you're not 100% satisfied with the results!

Order now while supplies last!

When to use persuasive writing

People often use persuasive writing to convince the reader to buy something. That could be a vacation, a new type of drink, or a computer game.

Presenting persuasive writing

Try some persuasive writing. Write an advertisement, a poster, or a brochure, and make it as eye-catching as you can to grab the reader's attention.

- Use large and striking pictures.
- Vary the font size of your text.
- Write in the present tense to make it sound immediate and urgent.
- Use **positive** language that makes the reader think their life will be improved.

Word power

Choose your words carefully. Each word must make an impact. Rather than saying that something is "good," use words such as "amazing," "unique," "wonderful," "superb," "fantastic," and "one in a million."

- Use adjectives and superlatives—words such as "idyllic" and "outstanding."
- Present opinions as facts: "Mrs. Goochi says, 'This is the best handbag ever!'"
- Use phrases such as "leading experts agree," "leader in the field recommends," and "endorsed by" to show that something has been evaluated by an expert.
- Use technical or scientific words that sound authoritative, even though the reader won't understand them.

Use your computer to make a poster that looks really professional. Make your text different colors and fonts, and vary the font size. You could advertise one of the following or invent your own product:

- A vacation destination
- A hair product
- An environmentally-friendly car

Springboard

JUMPIN' BEENS

Live in concert
one chance in a million to see the stars perform!

ONE NIGHT ONLY
May 8th

The Dance Center is proud to present the sensational Jumpin'Beens performing hits from their latest album, Tweenie Beenies

"Tweenie Beenies, with its unique mix of up-beat backing tracks and amazing lyrics, is a winner...the best album to hit the music scene in years." Music Review

To buy tickets, visit www.jumpinbeens.com or call The Dance Center at (818) 555-3100

Put the most important information at the top.

Provide a quote to back up your statement.

Give purchase details at the bottom of the poster.

INFORMATIVE WRITING

Imagine you've been asked to write a report about animals of the rain forest. It's a topic that interests you, but you don't know much about it. Where do you start? Do you want your report to be about just mammals or all sorts of different animals including insects, reptiles, and birds?

ACTIVITY

Have a brainstorming session with a group of friends. Write "rain forest animals" in the middle of a large sheet of paper. Then write the names of rain forest animals and what you know about each one. On another sheet of paper, list the things that you need to research, such as: What other mammals live in the rain forest? Are there any rain forest insects?

Researching

Find out about your topic using reference books and the Internet. If you're using reference books, use the contents page and index to speed up your research.
Scan the text for key words:
"Poison dart frogs are brightly colored. Their coloring is a warning to other animals that they are poisonous."
Take notes. Write down only the words that are important, like "frilly lizard = green, eats mosquitoes, hibernates."

What we know
Monkeys, toucans, and frogs live in the rain forest.

What we need to find out
What is a rain forest/Where is it found? (for intro)
Insects
Reptiles
Other mammals

Starting to write

Organize your writing into sections so that, for example, all your information on toucans is under the same section.
• Use a subheading for each section.
• Write in the present tense because you are describing the way the animals are.
• Move from the general to the specific, for example "Monkeys communicate with each other by making loud noises. Howler monkeys are the loudest monkeys of all."

Useful words

Use words that relate to your chosen topic to make your writing sound accurate and factual. For example, for a project on rain forest animals, the following words would be useful: canopy, camouflage, extinction, leaf litter, and species.

Use technical words, such as "habitat," "herbivores," and "primates."

Start with general information.

Tip
You don't have to arrange the sections of your report in any particular order because they are not linked in a sequence.

Use adjectives to describe the animals, such as "black" or "hairy."

Gorilla

The gorilla's habitat is in forested areas of Africa. They are the largest of the primates, which are the group of animals that include monkeys, apes, and humans.

Use subheadings to divide up the text.

Description

Gorillas have black or dark red hair. The adult male gorilla is called a silverback because the hair along his back turns gray.

Pick out an interesting piece of information and place it in a box outside the main text.

Lifespan
Gorillas live up to 30 years.
Food
Gorillas are herbivores. They eat:
o fruit
o leaves
o stems of plants

Illustrate your text with photos and labeled drawings.

Write a caption underneath each illustration.

The gorilla is an intelligent animal.

PROJECT WRITING: ANCIENT GREECE

Suppose you have been asked to write about Ancient Greece. Before narrowing down that topic, do general research about Ancient Greece—from its inventors, thinkers, writers, and poets to its architecture, the city-state, and daily life.

What interests you the most?

Get ideas through a brainstorming session and make a list of things to include, such as farming, gods, festivals, medicine, and myths. Organize your ideas into an idea web with one detail, such as "homes" or "food" in the center. Write down related key words around it.

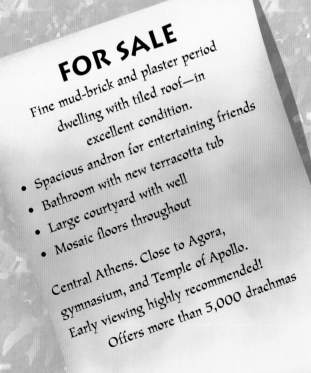

figs and grapes

fish and seafood

wheat and barley

Food

goat

bread

olives

milk and chees[e]

FOR SALE

Fine mud-brick and plaster period dwelling with tiled roof—in excellent condition.

- Spacious andron for entertaining friends
- Bathroom with new terracotta tub
- Large courtyard with well
- Mosaic floors throughout

Central Athens. Close to Agora, gymnasium, and Temple of Apollo. Early viewing highly recommended!

Offers more than 5,000 drachmas

Which style?

When you have enough information, think about the different ways in which you could present it. For example:

- Newspaper report from *The Sparta Daily News* on the invention of the water clock
- Interview with Alexander the Great
- Advertisement for an Ancient Greek home
- Balanced report on whether girls should go to school or not
- Sports report on the Olympic Games
- A letter from a Greek child to their best friend

Daily life in Ancient Greece

The houses in Ancient Greece usually consisted of two or three rooms built around a courtyard. A wealthy home might have two courtyards and an upstairs floor. The courtyard was the most important part of the home. That is where the family gathered to talk, entertain friends, and listen to stories.

Children in Ancient Greece played with many different toys. Favorite toys were rattles, wooden hoops, toy animals, dolls made from clay, yo-yos, and a horse on wheels that was pulled along. Children also enjoyed outdoor games such as juggling and playing on seesaws.

The Ancient Greeks loved to tell and listen to stories. They told many stories about their gods and goddesses and how the world was created. The most famous storytellers were the blind poet Homer and the slave Aesop, whose fables are still read today.

The Ancient Greeks ate a lot of vegetables and fresh fruit, such as grapes and figs. They made bread from wheat and barley and kept goats to use their milk, which they made cheese with. If they lived near the coast, they ate fish and seafood. They did not eat meat.

Clothes were made from linen and wool. They consisted of a piece of cloth wrapped around the body and held together with pins and brooches. They wore sandals or went barefoot.

ACTIVITY

Turn this page of information into a report. How can you write it so that it is easy to read, informative, and eye-catching?

Remember to :
- use subheadings
- put some text in boxes
- use bullet points and labels
- illustrate your writing with drawings or diagrams
- give each illustration a caption

SUMMING UP

There are many ways to write and present nonfiction texts. They include news reports, balanced reports, informative writing, and project writing.

Checklist

Here is a list of things to remember when writing nonfiction.

• Audience/purpose

Before you start, you should have some idea who you are writing for. Is your writing intended for a friend, a teacher, or someone you don't know? The language you use will depend on the audience.

• Presentation

The way you present your writing is important and will vary. If you are recounting the details of a trip, you should follow the sequence of events. If you are writing a report for a newspaper, you should put the most important facts at the beginning.

• Facts and opinions

Nonfiction is primarily about facts, but it can also include opinions. Make sure that you distinguish between the two and don't present opinions as facts.

• Research

Make sure your facts are accurate. **Double-check** information you find on the Internet.

Don't forget to:

Take notes
• Have a brainstorming session to collect ideas.
• Use an idea web, time line, or another kind of diagram to structure your argument.

Organize your facts
• Start with a heading.
• Use subheadings when you start a new topic.
• Use bullet points to list facts.

Illustrate your work
Include drawings, diagrams, and charts to support your information.

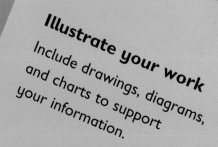

Get together with your friends to produce a school or class newspaper. It's a good idea to have one or two people in charge of each page. You could include pages on:

- school news
- other news
- sports
- book reviews
- puzzles
- interviews

Springboard 1

Springboard 2

Organize a book club and ask each member to write a review of a book they've read. Keep the reviews in a folder or post them on your school's Web site, so that others can read them when they're looking for a good book.

Springboard 3

With a group, write a reference book about a topic in which you are all interested. Pair off, then have each pair write two pages on a particular aspect of the topic. For example, you might write a book about rock bands with sections about:

- when did rock start?

- survey of favorite rock bands

- balanced debate: is listening to music while doing homework helpful or harmful?

- in-depth look at one band

- the best guitarist / drummer / singer

THE DRUMBEATS

GLOSSARY

Active voice shows that the subject of a sentence is doing the action

Alliteration when words begin with the same sound for effect

Article a piece of nonfiction writing about a topic in a newspaper or magazine

Bold type that has thick, heavy lines

Caption writing that explains an illustration or photo

Chronological order events set out in the order that they happened

Colloquial informal expressions and phrases used in conversation

Column a piece of writing that is set to a narrow width. Newspapers are laid out in columns

Contraction two words that are shortened, using an apostrophe in place of one or more letters

Controversial a matter or event that people strongly disagree about

Double-check to check a fact twice, using a second source of reference

Draft a first try at writing something

Edit change a piece of text to improve it

Explanatory clause part of a sentence that gives extra information

Fiction a story about made-up characters and situations

Font the style of type used

Glossary a list explaining difficult or technical words, which is arranged in alphabetical order and placed near the end of the book

Headline title of a newspaper article

Impersonal language written in the third person

Index an alphabetical list of subjects that can be found in the main text

Metaphor a phrase which says one thing *is* another but isn't literally true, such as "Sue's a mouse". Sue isn't actually a mouse but might be shy or nervous like a mouse

Paragraph a section of several sentences about a subject

Passive voice shows what is being done to the subject of a sentence

Plot the events that determine what a story is about

Positive emphasizing what is good

Questionnaire a list of questions to be filled out by people, to gather information

Quote the exact words that a person has spoken

Recount retelling of events in the order that they happened

Resume a record that lists your education and achievements

Review an account of a book, film, DVD, play, or piece of music that gives the writer's opinion

Scan reading a piece of text quickly to find out the key ideas or words

Simile a phrase that compares one thing to another using the words "like" or "as," such as "Hard as nails"

Spell-check a computer program that checks and corrects spelling

Statement sentence that gives facts and/or personal opinion

Subheading a title that has less importance than a heading

Summary a brief account giving the main points of a piece of information

Survey finding out opinions on a particular issue

INDEX

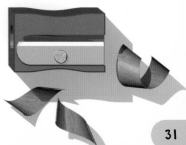

NOTES FOR PARENTS AND TEACHERS

- Explain the purpose of organizational features in a reference book—the contents page (says what the book is about), the index (provides a list of words, arranged alphabetically, and gives relevant page numbers), and glossary (explains difficult and/or technical words).

- Encourage your child to ask questions about natural phenomena—such as why the sky is blue, why grass is green, and why the days are shorter in the winter —and to use reference books to find the answers.

- Help your child to write and produce a newsletter, turning daily events at home and at school into news items. Remind him or her to use newspaper features, such as a headline and byline, and to set their writing in narrow columns. The newsletter could also incorporate a sports article, advertisements, a weather report, and even a simple crossword puzzle.

- With your child, look at advertisements in newspapers and on TV. Check for persuasive language and make a list of words that are often used. You could also put together a scrapbook of headlines from newspapers and ask your child to point out the ones they find most effective, giving reasons for their choices.

- Together, make up catchy headlines that use alliteration to grab the reader's attention.

- Develop your child's observational skills by collecting a variety of different leaves and asking the child to draw each leaf as accurately as possible. Have him or her write a simple caption to accompany each drawing.

- Talk to your child about creatures found in or near the home—for example, spiders, ants, and birds. Encourage him or her to research each animal in reference books and on the Internet. Then have him or her write a fact sheet about each creature, giving information about lifespan, habitat, and feeding habits.

- Encourage your child to draw an animal in its natural environment and to write a caption with an interesting piece of information about the animal. Point out that the drawing should be as realistic as possible.

- Encourage your child to keep a notebook in which he or she writes down observations about their surroundings. Points of interest could include tree species in the area, the sky and cloud formations, canals, rivers, and lakes. As an extension to this activity, he or she could add observations of the seasons changing.

- Together, find topics for debate that are centered around daily life, for example arguments for and against who should take the dog for a walk, who should be in charge of the cleaning, or whether video games should be regarded as leisure activities or tools for learning.

- Encourage your child to keep records of special days or outings. Keep these records in a folder so that the child has a log of some of the things he or she did in a given year.

- With your child, prepare interview questions to ask a family member or a friend. Questions could be about a recent vacation, hobbies, or their favorite time of the year.

- Together, prepare a list of interview questions intended for your child's favorite author. Questions could relate to the author's life, his or her writing process, or a particular book's plots, and characters.

- Initiate a discussion with your child about a recent film, play, or book. Ask about likes and dislikes. Encourage your child to support his or her opinions.

- Encourage your child to keep a diary of daily events.